An Elementary School Text of the Holy Christian Bible

Mario E. Lombardo

"An Elementary School Text of the Holy Christian Bible," by Mario E. Lombardo. ISBN 978-1-63868-204-2 (softcover).

Published 2025 by Virtualbookworm.com Publishing, Inc., P.O. Box 9949, College Station, TX 77842, US. ©2025, Mario E. Lombardo. All rights reserved. No part of this publication may be reproduced, stored in a retrieval system, or transmitted in any form or by any means, electronic, mechanical, recording or otherwise, without the prior written permission of Mario E. Lombardo.

"Start children off on the way they should go, and even when they are old they will not turn from it."

Proverbs 22.6

Reading this little booklet, you will learn the answers to these questions about the Christian religion.

What is the Bible?

What story is in the Bible?

What are the important teachings of the Bible?

WHAT IS THE BIBLE?

The Bible is the best-selling and most-read book in the world.

It consists of two parts.

The first part is called the Old Testament.

And the second part is called the New Testament.

The Bible is more than 2,000 years old.

WHAT STORY IS IN THE OLD TESTAMENT?

In the Old Testament, the first story is about God creating the world we live in.

God first created the earth, the oceans and rivers, the sun, the moon, a sky filled with stars, and His Home in Heaven.

God filled the earth with plants and animals, the oceans and rivers with fish, and the sky with birds.

God next created the first man named Adam and the first woman named Eve.

God blew his breath on them and Adam and Eve came alive.

This breath of life is called the soul.

The soul is invisible like air and, like air, it is needed to keep our bodies alive.

It took six days for God to create the world.

God made the seventh day a Holy Day and a day of rest.

Today, the seventh day is called Sunday.

After God created Adam and Eve, He placed them in Eden.

Eden had a garden with a lot of different plants and fruit trees growing in it.

God told Adam and Eve they could eat any food in the garden, except fruit from a special tree growing there.

But Adam and Eve did

not obey God and they each ate the fruit from that special tree.

God was angry with Adam and Eve for disobeying him.

Disobeying God is called a sin.

As the years passed, more and more people were living on Earth.

Some believed in God and some were non-believers.

One of the most important believers was Abraham, a religious leader with many followers.

Abraham loved God, and prayed often to Him.

God often spoke to Abraham.

Abraham always listened to God and did what God asked him to do.

Abraham was troubled by people who sinned.

Moses was another religious man who loved God and who also was upset with sinners.

So, Abraham and Moses prayed to God, asking Him to help the sinners.

God answered their prayers by giving Moses a stone tablet that had ten rules written on it.

The rules stated how God expected us to behave.

God promised that if we follow the rules, we will get to live with Him in heaven.

These rules are called the Ten Commandments.

Two of these Commandments told us the "right" kind of behavior He expected of us.

The first one told us to "Remember to keep Sunday holy" and the second one told us to "Honor [our] father and mother."

The other eight Commandments listed the "wrong" kinds of behavior (or sins).

For example, one of them said "You shall not steal" and another said "You shall not kill."

Abraham and Moses were upset because too many people were still not obeying the Commandments.

Now, there were many other holy men in the Old Testament's story who were also upset by sinners not obeying God's Commandments.

Some of these holy men were called Prophets.

Isaiah was one of the prophets.

Isaiah, like Abraham and Moses, also saw that too many people were not obeying God's rules

so he prayed to God
asking for help.

A loving and caring God
answered Isaiah's
prayers.

God gave the prophet
Isaiah a special power to
see the future.

This is what Isaiah saw:
that God would be
sending His Son to Earth
with a plan to forgive
sinners. This plan of
forgiveness is called
Confession.

The story ends in the
Old Testament with the
hope that Isaiah's vision
would come true.

WHAT STORY IS IN THE NEW TESTAMENT?

The story begins with God sending the Holy Spirit to a holy woman named Mary to help her birth a son.

Her son was born on Christmas and was named Jesus.

Jesus grew up as a man like all other men.

However, Jesus was also the Son of God.

Many people refused to believe Jesus was the Son of God even though he did deeds that only God could do.

Deeds called miracles, such as, making a blind person see, or a deaf person hear, or a dead person come alive again.

News of these deeds quickly spread throughout the land, increasing the number of believers of Jesus being the Son of God.

Jesus then chose twelve of these believers to follow Him. These twelve holy men were called Disciples.

Jesus loved the Disciples who followed Him everywhere listening to His teachings and seeing His many miracles.

Now Jesus knew his final hour on Earth was ending, so He told the Disciples that God would forgive sinners who confessed sins and were sorry.

He then told them He would be put to death by non-believers, but would rise from the grave on the third day after He was buried.

And that is exactly what happened to Jesus.

Wicked non-believers mocked and made fun of Him, made him carry a heavy wooden cross, and then nailed his hands and feet to the cross.

They left Jesus hanging and suffering on the cross until he died.

Jesus was then buried in a sealed tomb.

Three days after He was buried, the tomb was discovered empty.

Jesus had arisen from the grave just as He had told his Disciples.

This act of Jesus rising from his grave, and then appearing in person before his Disciples, proved He was truly the son of God and is celebrated by Christians every year on Easter Sunday.

The story ends in the New Testament with God sending the Holy Spirit to bring Jesus Home.

His purpose on Earth was finished.

WHAT ARE IMPORTANT TEACHINGS OF THE BIBLE?

Important teachings of the Bible are:

- There is only one God.

- He created the world and its people.

- He sent His Son, Jesus, to save our souls.

- Jesus suffered and died for our sins.

- God's plan to save our souls included confession for the forgiveness of sins.

- The Ten Commandments tell us how to be good Christians.

A FINAL PERSONAL NOTE

REMEMBER: If we love God and Jesus, we will live with them in a joyful Heaven.

"Fathers, ... bring them [children] up in the training and instruction of the Lord."

Ephesians 6.4

"Let the little children come to me, and do not hinder them, for the Kingdom of God belongs to such as these."

Mark 10.14

RESPECTFUL APPRECIATION

Sincere thanks to Robert Hardiman, Tom Shipley, and Shirley Wind, each of whom reviewed the manuscript and provided valued insights and suggestions.

NOTES

www.ingramcontent.com/pod-product-compliance
Lightning Source LLC
Chambersburg PA
CBHW061316040426
42444CB00010B/2678